I See God

by Avi Gardner

Illustrations by Karen Hinojosa · Cover Art by Iris Schille

Dedicated to my nieces, Darcey and Caroline.

WestBow Press books may be ordered through booksellers or by contacting:

WestBow Press
A Division of Thomas Nelson & Zondervan
1663 Liberty Drive
Bloomington, IN 47403
www.westbowpress.com
844-714-3454

Illustrations by Karen Hinojosa
Cover art by Iris Schille
Book layout by Kristen Ferris

Font Design copyright © P.L.Digital, Inc., data copyright Projective Solutions, Inc., additional data copyright Type Solutions, Inc. Portions Copyright 1994 Microsoft Corporation. All rights reserved.

ISBN: 978-1-9736-9571-4 (sc)
ISBN: 978-1-9736-9572-1 (e)

Library of Congress Control Number: 2020912018

Print information available on the last page.

WestBow Press rev. date: 11/13/2020

WESTBOW
PRESS®
A DIVISION OF THOMAS NELSON
& ZONDERVAN

I see God in everything I do

I see God shine in me and you

I see God in the stars

I feel God from afar.

I see God in everything I do

I feel God everywhere I am

I see God shining in the sand

I see God in the moon

I feel God coming soon

18

I see God everywhere I am

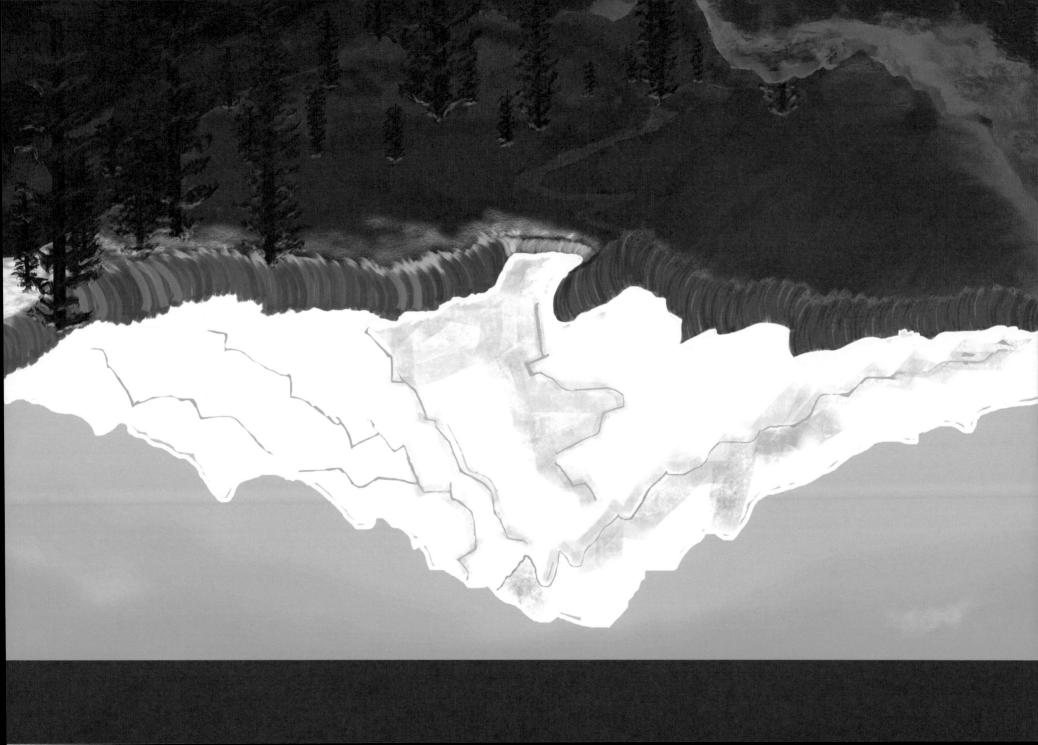

I see God in everything I do

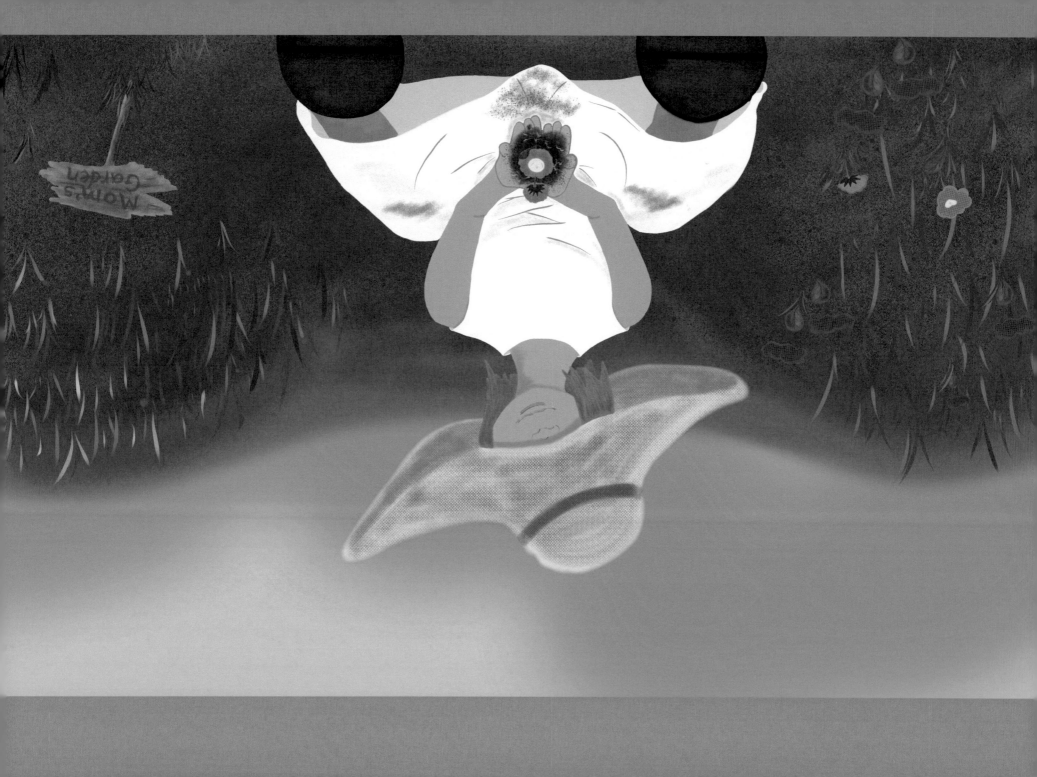

I see God shine in me and you

I see God in the stars

I feel God from afar.

I see God in everything I do

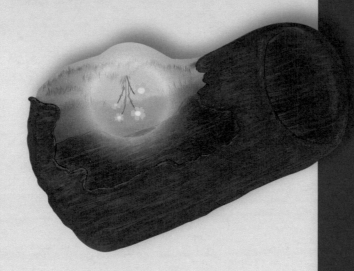

Find the song on iTunes:
itunes.apple.com/us/album/i-see-god-single/1455176367

To see more go to:
www.avigardner.com

I See God
lyrics

I see God in everything I do
I see God shine in me and you
I see God in the Stars
I feel God from afar
I see God in everything I do

~~~

I feel God everywhere I am
I see God shining in the sand
I see God in the moon
I feel God coming soon
I see God everywhere I am

~~~

I see God in everything I do
I see God shine in me and you
I see God in the stars
I feel God from afar
I see God in everything I do

Printed in the United States
By Bookmasters